Leaving

and

Cleaving:

The Biblical Guide to a Happy Marriage

Dell Belew, PhD

Copyright © by Dell Belew, PhD 2020

Cross image from Clipart

Leaving and Cleaving: The Biblical Guide to a Happy Marriage
By Dell Belew, PhD.

Other books by Dell Belew

The Woman, The Red Dragon, and The End of the Age

Traveling Light in Times of Darkness

Son Rise Reflections

A Stitch in Time: A Supplemental Writing Text

From Legos to Logos: Building a Discourse

The Fine Art of Worship I (Color), II (B/W)

The Woman and Her Seed

The Undiet Book

Healing: Miracle or Mystery?

Who is the Holy Ghost?

In Full Bloom: Poems from a Full Life

Firewalker: A Novel

Art: The Language of the Soul

Meditations: Living the Word Daily

The Princess Dell Journals

Money, Money, Money: Its Roots and Fruits

Prayer Gardening: Planting/Harvesting a Fruitful Prayer Life

The Blood: The River Flowing from Calvary

Published in the United States of America by

Genesis One Designs Publishing: www.dellbelew.com

ISBN:

Table of Contents

Dedication

I dedicate this book to the glory of God for he has brought me to this place and called me to teach and counsel. I dedicate this book also to the couples who have honored me by asking me to officiate over their marriages. May they rest in the peace of knowing that their Divine Counselor is overseeing their relationships through all of life's joys and sorrows as long as they both shall live. Amen!

Rules for Marriage

Say I love you

Tell the truth

Forgive

Don't bring up the past

Be romantic

Keep your promises

Laugh together

Compliment each other

Enjoy each other

Unknown author.

$\mathcal{I}ntroduction$

""For this reason a man will leave his father and mother and be united [cleave] to his wife, and the two will become one flesh" (Eph. 5:31 NIV).

This verse in Ephesians is where I get my title. The KJV uses "cleave," thus the title *Leaving and Cleaving.*

Long before the Bible was written down, the God of the Universe had some guidance about what constitutes marriage and about how it should be implemented. As an ordained minister, I have officiated/blessed many marriages. The first thing I insist upon is counseling both with the couple together and at least one session with the individuals before I will ask God to bless the marriage.

This text is a reference guide provided for the couple to take home after the first counseling session. They are expected to read and come prepared for the next sessions with questions and comments. Of all of the couples whose marriages I have officiated only two have ended, sad to say.

I've officiated in churches and chapels, hotel ballrooms, backyard balconies, private living rooms, gazebos at Cypress Gardens in SC, and on the bluff of coastal Georgia rivers. The locations seem to have nothing to do with the longevity of the marriages, but I believe the couple's dedication to keeping the commandments of God has everything to do with happy marriages.

With that in mind, I offer these words from God's Word and his will.

--Rev. Dr. Dell Belew

What Difference Does It Make?

Eric Metaxas recently had a guest on his radio show who is the CEO of *Communio*, a nonprofit organization that goes to churches to teach them how to strengthen and minister to married couples, and, therefore, families. The CEO, JP Gance, stated, "Marriage is the root of so much social decline."

While that is a startling conclusion, I believe it is uncomfortably true. The one fact we can all agree on is that the family breakdown is evident I the social environment in addictions, sexual and physical abuse, suicides, the breakdown of education, and many more too numerous to mention.

The breakdown of the family begins with the breakdown of marriages and the dramatic change in how we define marriage and the looseness with which we regard morals. All told, the very definition of and sanctity of marriage has redefined our social fabric all the way from the manner in which children behave to the sexual mores of adults. Teachers cannot teach children who have no discipline at home; when the children are gathered together, that lack of discipline spreads to others in the room.

However, as much as I would like to write the book as a social and political treatise on what's wrong with our world, I am specifically charged with making sure that couples who take the vows of marriage become part of the better statistics by teaching the basic tenets of the Biblical and Godly basis for a happy and healthy home to maintain and, hopefully, correct our society from the inside out, especially the Christian portion of it. I sincerely hope to bring back some sense of decency and hope to a nation that has lost sight of what is good and Godly—knowing that He who made us knows what is best and has written it all down for us to use as a guide.

*   *   *

Over the centuries of human interaction, many things have changed depending largely on the cultures and world events. Our twenty-first-century concept of marriage is quite skewed—even within the Christian church. This should not be, especially given the fact that marriage is both spiritual and physical in purpose and human relationships.

The rituals of marriage have changed dramatically reflecting the change in purpose and importance. Presently, marriage is like a side dish at the relationship table, so people tend to neglect it and, along with it, the right and wrong way to engage with other people.

I am just going to jump right into this discussion and say that the purpose of marriage is to join two people to work together and for procreation. In order to procreate, the couple must be male and female given that each has a part in the creation of the child.

On a purely physical level, God put a chemical/hormone in a woman that is released when she is ovulating. This secretion can be detected by the male usually through her urine, which is why men and women who share the same bathroom (or whatever facility where this was done in centuries past). While I am not making this stuff up, you can check with Google about the facts. Not to belittle our sex drives, but this same chemical is secreted by animals to attract other animals of the same species. We often express it by saying that the animal/she is in "heat." That is another way of saying that she is ovulating.

Getting back to the human sex regarding what is happening in sex, don't be shocked when I say that having sex with a partner of the opposite sex is a union that creates a soul tie, the second reason for being of the opposite sex. Our Creator made humans to function whereas the joining together of a man and woman puts the original "man" or "adam" back together. One without the other cannot reach his/her full potential. When God created an apple, for example, he put seeds in it to create more apples and seeds.

People who have many sex partners are really confused spiritually because of the many soul ties he/she has created through sex. I'm saying all of that to say that before a person can be sexually united with his/her mate, there needs to be a spiritual breaking of those ties. Without that, the couple (possibly) brings many people to the marriage bed. Any minister officiating at the wedding should know how to break those soul ties, and I recommend that be done before the wedding.

While I am on this subject, let me address the past lives of the partners. In our time, it is more prevalent that neither one of the couple is a virgin, sadly. For this reason, I do not recommend that couples share their *past* sexual encounters or practices with their intended partner. This may seem to be bad advice that leads people to think I am encouraging dishonesty in the relationship. I am not suggesting they lie to one another, but simply withhold information that may affect the present relationship.

If the couple already has knowledge of each of their past sexual lives, there might already have been issues that came to the surface. What one person has done before entering into a new relationship is no one's business unless the former relationship has caused medical (physical or emotional) problems that need to be addressed (i.e., STDs).

The problems that need to be addressed may be emotional problems related to guilt, shame, or anger toward the person or persons with whom they had sex. Entering into a new marital relationship with emotional or physical baggage related to sex can wreck the partnership. In counseling, I am available for private consultation when these issues are looming over the couple.

Union of the two souls begins with the sexual union. After God created Adam (in Hebrew "man"), he saw that it was not good that man should be "alone." That word in Hebrew is "bad" (905 Strong's) related to the word "badad" (909 Strong's) that means solitary or alone.

I would like to suggest that what that means is that God saw that man should not be solitary or one being within himself. I say that because of what God did was to divide the man's parts into two. It doesn't take a scientific mind to understand that God was not just giving the man a "partner" to keep him company; he was literally taking parts out of the adam in order to perform certain tasks, in this case, procreation.

Forget all that mumbo-jumbo about how God took Eve out of Adam's side so she could be alongside him. That is true on some level, but the truth is that he took the womb out of Adam and fashioned another being so that together they would work the Garden and multiply (i.e., procreate). If we ever needed a good reason to negate same-sex marriage, this is it! This is also a great place to shout!

We often interpret God's saying that man should not be "alone" to mean that man without a partner would be lonely or a solitary soul. While that is true, it does not convey the correct problem. Adam needed someone who could not only tend the Garden but replenish it with another man (a womb-man).

Although this might be stretching the point unnecessarily, God put seeds in fruit so they could multiply. He had Noah take 2 of some of the animals on the ark so they could replenish the earth after the flood. Noah and his children, the same. For those who choose not to believe the Bible, this point will be a stretch though it is a natural fact that it takes one male sperm and one female egg to produce another human being.

After God took the womb out of the man to create a womb-man, Adam received her as his own flesh and bones. That is forever what happens in the birth of a child; the child is a union of their parents. But before that child can multiply, he/she must also procreate. Procreation cannot happen between people of the same sex. The subjects of adoption, in vetro fertilization (IVF), or other forms do not come into this discussion in the way of "having" children, so I am going to leave that discussion here.

That's being the case, God further explains, "Therefore shall a man leave his father and his mother, and shall cleave unto his wife: and they shall be one flesh" (Gen. 2:24 KJV). "Cleave" is a somewhat archaic word for "unite" or "join," but it works better for my title! The union of marriage is both physical and spiritual, as I have said previously.

I am going out on a limb here and say this union is not possible between same sex partners. I know there are other means of having sex, but it is not the same as the Biblical "going into her" that constitutes marriage and certainly will not result in bearing children. Technically, civil services do not constitute marriage except from a legal standpoint. It is the sexual union of a man and woman that constitutes marriage and at the same time makes procreation possible.

Never in the history of man has a man had a baby; they do not have the necessary equipment. The only "man" to do so was a woman who maintained her "equipment" in her new relationship as a man. Quarrel if they must, but the arguments of the LGBTQ community do not change the facts.

In the Bible, sex is generally referred to in marriage as "going in unto her" and refers to carnal knowledge as well as spiritual covenants between males and females who each have the physical elements to make procreation possible: "21 And Jacob said unto Laban, Give me my wife, for my days are fulfilled, that I may go in unto her'" (Gen. 29:21 KJV). We call these "soul ties." There was no civil ceremony as such—just the spiritual and sexual communion in this case between Jacob and Leah [not his love, Rachel.] A feast was usually celebrated.

Before I leave the subject of these verses in Genesis, let me deal with the fact that when two opposite sex people say their vows before Almighty God, they do so vowing to live together in "holy" matrimony, in sickness and in health, for richer or for poorer for as long as they both shall live; they make these vows before God and the witnesses gathered.

These words are not taken seriously in the modern world. Divorce rates are amazingly high even among Christians who vowed before God to stay together. We cannot talk about marriage in the modern world without discussing divorce.

I recommend couples go to the following site for some staggering statistics compiled by the Wilkinson & Finkbeiner Family Law Attorneys: https://www.wf-lawyers.com/divorce-statistics-and-facts/. After reading through a very long list of factors pertaining to divorce, you should get some idea why counseling and giving much consideration to all of the factors in your decision to marry are mandatory for success in life with a marriage partner. I will be discussing children later, but for now let me say that children deserve to get a good start in life in a loving home.

Being a divorce statistic myself, I can testify to the deep sorrow experienced by everyone in a family. This fact makes me a better candidate for marriage counseling because I have seen so many of the factors listed on the website both personally and from other couples' issues.

The Hand that Rocks the Cradle

In counseling sessions, children would not be treated this soon, but because of the discussion regarding procreation, I think it might be a good place.

In the modern concept of marriage and families, the introduction of children into the union of two people anticipating a marriage is prevalent. One young man who had reached his late 30s without finding a mate, expressed his chief concern because the eligible women he had met all seem to have children either from a previously relationship out of wedlock or a previous marriage. Naturally, reaching the age of 37 or 38, he would want children but was sorrowful that they might not be his own biological offspring.

Not to cast negativity over the people who come into a first, second, or third marriage, children do present many factors that require an intelligent and emotional reckoning before two people commit to joining in holy matrimony.

First, let us consider the conversation a couple might have before marriage where children are not involved beforehand. It is a conversation that must take place rather than one of those surprise discussions when the lifetime commitment has been made during the ceremony. I know, personally, of couples who discover into the marriage that one of them is adamantly opposed to having children, a point possibly not revealed knowing the other might not enter into the marriage if he/she knew. It is wrong to assume the other partner might change his/her mind. Having children is a very emotional aspect of a marriage relationship and should not be entered into lightly. It may be true that love covers a multitude of sins, but it cannot cover a partner's desire or need to have children. In the 21st century, there are ways to plan for having or not having children unlike our parents' lifetime.

The marriage counseling session could be a place for a couple to discuss the reasons children are important to one or both of the partners. If the discussion needs to take place later, make sure to contact a counselor rather than making emotional decisions that might come back to haunt you. Raising children is not for sissies because parental responsibility for creating the next generation is paramount to good societies and cultures.

In his 1865 poem "The Hand that Rocks the Cradle is the Hand that Rules the World," William Ross Wallace praises the power of the individual who is responsible for rearing the children. In today's society that hand might be that of the father who made the choice to stay home while the wife earns a living. In either case, one parent should be rocking the cradle—and not that of a stranger or daycare worker.

I am getting onto my soap box now, but when a parent turns over his/her child to another person, he/she is giving permission for a stranger to impart his/her stamp on their personality and social behavior (and sometimes that stamp might be a group effort, further confusing the matter of a child's sense of well-being and discipline.)

I will resist going into my full discussion regarding the emotional and intellectual development of children, but let me say that for two people who chose to have children to then turn them over to strangers for that development hasn't thought through how strange and negative that outcome might be. This education would be "herd mentality" at best. That also includes a steady diet of television or internet "education." Parents will be held accountable someday for what they provide or allow their children to be exposed.

Stepping into Parenthood

Step-parenting can be a difficult task for so many reasons that it may not be fruitful to open that can here. However, couples considering marriage have to know on some levels what they are getting into.

Let me first say that whatever a partner says or does BEFORE marriage may not represent what occurs AFTER the marriage. Sometimes people even misrepresent themselves to make a marriage happen. We often convince ourselves that we can or will do whatever it takes to make the marriage partner happy, but that can change when reality sets in. The "other" parent has a major role in how this goes down, so they somehow have to be on board with whatever is decided or considered.

There are as many scenarios for this discussion as there are people to have it. Taking first the woman who has a child or children when she begins to date her chosen mate; if she cares about her children, she will be watching carefully to determine how the mate handles them—I really mean "handles." How does he or she respond to them when they are present? What about that pleases or disturbs you—you should be asking? The signs might not be as obvious when you are star struck, but future "handling" is there. His/her own siblings and parents might be a clue. How does he/she treat his mother, for example.

This is a good place to quote Maya Angelou who said, "When he [the date per se] shows you what he's about, believe him." We are too often busy thinking about our relationship with the other person that we lose sight of that person's possible relationship to other humans, very important humans at that!

Before marriage when "other" children are involved, the first consideration beyond the emotional bond is who will discipline the children? And how will the discipline be handled? It should be a couple's decision apart from the immediate need to do so. No matter to whom the children "belong," the couple should be on the same team. Children who encounter conflict about the way they are being raised can/will use that to their advantage and wreak havoc in a family. More importantly, the child's confidence in himself/herself will often undergo dramatic shifts with sometimes poor outcomes.

Under no circumstance should the children hear negative conversations about their "other" parent (i.e., the ex husband/wife) regardless of which parent it is about. Children did not ask to come into the world and certainly did not ask to be plunged into a war zone where the individual parents have chosen their fellow soldiers against the other. Children should be shielded against ex-couple's battles at all costs.

Another aspect of stepchildren involves both partners having children from previous relationships. I have seen it work out very well; more often than not, it becomes an all-out tug of war on many levels. Mature adults should know how to work through these mixed parenting situations but many do not. Adults often use their children to get even with the ex; however, parents should never run down the other parent or his/her choice of a new mate. It keeps children from responding to the step parents in a positive way. This also affects the children's personality growth in the family and in society. There is a wonderful poem entitled, "Children Learn what They Live," by Dorothy Law Nolte. One portion is appropriate here: "If children live with criticism, they learn to condemn."

As I said, parenting isn't for sissies. We may not be perfect, but we can learn to talk and act in a way that is proper once we learn how to do it. Learn patience with step children and give them love that heals the wounds they have probably brought into the new relationship. Teach them to love and respect you and your children.

Teach your own children the same for their step parent and his/her children. By all means, attempt to get along with the parent of your step children.

None of this is easy, but it is necessary for a successful relationship with your new mate and his/her children.

In the Bedroom

I got started talking about the importance of sex, but delayed the emphasis until I could discuss the procreation part of sex, which I remind you is the ultimate reason for marriage (i.e., sex) in the first place.

Sex and money are the two leading causes of divorce, I'm told. Although there are numerous reasons cited in the link I gave earlier, the root does seem to go back to these two.

So, let's consider how sex might be the fruit of a happy marriage. The sexual union between two consenting adults can be the highlight of an emotional and physical encounter. It is little wonder that sex is our connection to a soul. When it is good, it is very good.

However, when it is bad or wrong, it is very bad. Two things might top the list of "bad" sex: one is if it is not pleasing to one partner for reasons related to emotional or physical pain; the other is when one of the mates is unfaithful. Unfaithfulness with a partner outside of the marriage breaks the soul tie, resulting in emotional damage, the cause that might not even be known at the time. The ultimate emotional and spiritual results are too numerous to cover here, but they are usually deep.

The emotional bond between partners is broken; the repair is usually possible but not easy. This conundrum is the reason partners need to get counseling to break soul ties before they bring the previous partners into the marriage bed.

The second reason that sex could be a deal breaker for a marriage is discomfort or pain. For the number of people having sex, there are attitudes/desires for what happens in the bed. I am just going to drop this here and say that if one partner is uncomfortable with a sexual practice, he/she should say so and the other partner should make sure he/she does not force that practice. If the couple has not had sex already, this aspect of sex should be discussed. Couples should go into the marriage with love and understanding that sex is vital to a relationship. Sex is a subject too important to pass over lightly. By all means, let your partner know before and during sex; don't lie or pretend with something that could crash your marriage later.

One major sexual problem that I know about from talking to women is the refusal of one partner or the other to "allow" sex. There are as many reasons for a mate to refuse sex as there are people. Although they might seem valid, refusing sex may well push the other partner to seek it elsewhere.

Sexual need or desire is also different for most individuals, so taking that into consideration the understanding of human behavior on this topic may help. Let us first consider the Biblical advice from St. Paul concerning sexual relations in marriage:

Now for the matters you wrote about: "It is good for a man not to have sexual relations with a woman." 2 But since sexual immorality is occurring, each man should have sexual relations with his own wife, and each woman with her own husband. 3 The husband should fulfill his marital duty to his wife, and likewise the wife to her husband. 4 The wife does not have authority over her own body but yields it to her husband. In the same way, the husband does not have authority over his own body but yields it to his wife. 5 Do not deprive each other except perhaps by mutual consent and for a time, so that you may devote yourselves to prayer. Then come together again so that Satan will not tempt you because of your lack of self-control. (1 Cor. 7:1-5 NIV)

Sex is a powerful driving force in human behavior. The urge to have sex has a reasonable explanation: to draw two people of the opposite sex together for procreation. That's being the case, it becomes like any other necessary urge; it must be controlled. We could talk about the need to eat; the body is designed to become hungry in order to force the body to take care of itself. That is the subject of another book I have published, *The*

Undiet Book, so I will not mix subjects here except to say that sex has an enjoyable aspect that leads us to do what is necessary that we might otherwise reject or put off.

Some of you are scratching your heads while others are laughing that I compare eating food with sex. Trust me, the correlation is strong. Failure to engage in either has a damaging result to the body. But knowing how the spiritual aspect pertains to the physical is important.

Notice at end of the passage quoted, Paul tells us why withholding sex long term is a problem. Satan knows more than we do about sex and he waits at your bedside to see whether you will consent or deny. Denial, says Paul, will ultimately lead to the partner's search for another option.

The two options leading in popularity are adultery/fornication and/or pornography. Humans are not only fixated on sex but also Satan strongly encourages either or both. Prostitution, human trafficking, and pedophilia are the results of Satan's understanding of the human sexual drive, so they are also big business. He seizes on our sexual perversion and our greed.

Sex is not a bargaining tool and should never be used as such. If there is a physical problem, it should be dealt with immediately. If the reasons are psychological, they should be considered as well. I know women who hate sex for a variety of reasons and I cringe at the end result of their *refusal* to have sex with their husbands. However, this does not give a husband or wife permission to have adulterous relationships or, certainly, casual sex with someone other than his/her spouse.

These sexual relationship issues change for older couples. Supposedly, a man begins to lose his sexual drive at about 38 and then loses the ability sometime in his 50s. Women, on the other hand, become more sexually driven after 38 and, under most circumstances, will be able to "perform" on into their senior years. Therefore, older couples seeking to be married probably have greater reasons to have the sex talk so that problems of a physical nature do not become a problem. I suspect one of the reasons a woman's sex drive is greater after about 40 is that her child-bearing age is passing. I haven't seen any studies on this, so don't quote me!

The human body is a complex system of needs and desires, but Satan's rationale is quite on target. He is attempting to steal, kill, and destroy us by any means possible. So beware! Be on guard!

Money Can Buy Unhappiness

Given that money is one of the reasons for most divorces, it is important to talk about it before it becomes an issue. Each person should be open and above board about their salaries and indebtedness from the very beginning.

I decided when I was reading nineteenth-century literature in graduate school that the advent of the paycheck may be the first sign that money would be the downfall of the relationship between men and women.

In the nineteenth century in America during the Industrial Revolution, people (mostly men) began to leave home and the family farm to take jobs in factories, etc. I do not have any statistics about when actual money turned to paper checks for labor/wages, but I am sure that it became the outcome of men's no longer sharing in the family farm where everyone in the family shared the fruit of the harvest equally.

Psychologically, if the man's name is on the income, he might assume it is his. Most men, surely considered the money he brought home was for the purpose of housing, feeding, and clothing his family— and rightfully so. The women bore the children and cared for them just as she maintained the house and cooked the food as her part of the marriage contract.

In our culture, all of that has changed and so have the attitudes among men and women become skewed. The division of labor has shifted in some very odd ways even in my lifetime—having even begun in my early adult life with the women's liberation movement—but the subject is too complex to attempt a discussion here.

What I am trying to say, however, is that each person making the decision to join financial forces needs to consider where he or she stands regarding who will work where and how the money will be spent. These are not our daddies' rules any longer.

I'm jumping back on my soap box for this one. I am not only old-fashioned in my ideas but nature backs me up. Before children enter the picture, the discussion needs to involve them. They do not deserve to be put out to pasture while no one is home to raise them properly so they can grow up to be good social creatures who provide aid to their fellow man in creating a proper civilization. We are seeing the end result of women's having babies and then not training them or supervising them. Raising children with what I call "herd mentality" is wrong on so many levels. Look around our culture if you doubt what I'm saying.

I have written a long treatise on this subject elsewhere. These days we are not only carting them off to daycare where herd mentality is inadvertently taught but now we do the same when children get home. Children are encouraged to be glued to their tiny computers to give parents "me time."

Couples need to make the decision about how they want their children to grow up—it happens before we can barely turn around. My children are married and glued to their techy toys and I cringe. I miss them. . . .

Here is where the money comes into the decisions regarding children. Make financial arrangements for children when it comes to both parents' working schedule. If someone has to work to pay the bills, the other parent should be able to stay home and train them up in the way they should go—which also involves teaching them about the value of "things." Human interaction is a great learning tool, but too much interaction with people who are running about without much supervision is not the education children need.

Play time is time to learn how to be an adult. We are children for such a short amount of time, but we are adults for as much as 80 or 90 years. Play should be monitored as well. If it is chaotic or just wrong, it will follow the child into adulthood.

For a brief period of time, I put my son in a daycare that had come highly recommended. He was only there for 2 days a week. Into the second week, I picked him up as planned. He suddenly burst out, "'top runnin. Take a nap. 'top runnin'. Take a nap."

"What are you talking about?" I asked.

"That's what Ms. Ann says all day, 'top runnin,' Take a nap."

Although he was only 2 years old at the time, my son had found a way to express his anxiety over the confusion he experienced there. I took him out of there immediately. The moral to this story is listen to your children and take their distractions out of their hands if you need to allow them to express what they are experiencing. Waiting too long might be too late. I am right about this! Children are malleable but not for too long.

Do not misunderstand my warnings here. There is a large percentage of women and men who are dreadful parents so that daycare/othercare might be a blessing. For these and many other reasons, potential parents need to consider whether to have children and how they wish to train them. Science today helps us make choices our parents did not have—such as birth control.

Before I get too far astray, let me get back to the importance of play for a child. Childhood is practice for adulthood. One of my favorite past times was pretending to shop for groceries. My mother saved boxes and cans so I could have a good facsimile of groceries. Money and good grocery shopping techniques go hand-in-hand. I am a good grocery shopper today. (I also taught my dolls and stuffed animals while tapping on the wall as if it were a chalk board. I became a college professor.) I was getting groomed and prepared in my childhood to be a wise, practical, and socially responsible adult.

I also watched my parents regarding their money, its uses and the lack. I saw my mother "make do" with whatever was at her disposal and I learned. Giving children everything they want just to occupy them is giving them the wrong message.

This subject becomes a vital issue in making decisions about marriage. It does not always happen that each partner has the same family background regarding making and spending money. That can create problems, so talking them out before marriage is necessary. Having a plan about making and using money is fundamental to success.

My mother-in-law told me when my husband (her son!) came back from Viet Nam that we should pay our usual bills from his income and use mine for extras, vacations, and savings. That way, we would never depend on my income to survive so that I could quit when we decided to have children. That was very sound advice, but even then, two people have to decide exactly how that is going be done so the reasonable balance is not lost. I will add here that large purchases, anything from kitchen small appliances to houses, should be agreeable to each partner and the means by which they will be paid. Remember that a marriage is a partnership.

Couples are older in the 21st century before deciding to marry, so money handling has generally already been established individually. That makes this subject both critical and difficult. When couples marry, their credit scores/histories are joined. It might be a wise idea to wait until one or both credit ratings are good.

Questions to ask yourselves: Who will be the main "breadwinner"? If only one income, who will keep track? If two, how will the financial responsibilities be divided? How and how much will be set aside for savings and retirement? (Retirement will be very costly, so keep this in your savings future; it comes sooner than you think!) Word of advice: not only save at least 6-months of your average salary but do NOT keep it in funds that cannot be removed easily, like 401K's. Those are generally great earners in a good economy, but they move up and DOWN quickly when nationwide emergencies occur. In other words, do not be risky in your savings early on even if you have a lot of it. Because the experts recommend at least 6 months' salary in savings, that is a good prospective for the first years of marriage.

Banks presently are not paying much of anything for savings accounts, but they are safer initially. This is the voice of experience not only with my own but other people's financial situations. For further help, read my book *Money, Money, Money* available at Amazon.com and from me.

The couple needs to make a reasonable budget that includes paying off debts, saving, tithing, and economizing on spending until a good financial foundation has been established. Trust me, this situation will wreck your symbolic ship if you set sail without checking the weather and your sails, repairing them if necessary.

Another important decision that needs to be made is who will be handling the money and how. With online banking and debit spending come a whole host of problems from failing to tell the other when money is coming out of the account that could ultimately result in bank charges for overdrafts. Work out how that will be handled and who will balance the checkbook at the end of the month or keep a close watch on the online banking account. Determine a budget with each partner having certain spending cash so that debit cards do not become an issue.

But, as I said before, having separate accounts for budgeted items and another for personal use might be the best case. This system worked very well during one of my business ventures in which I took a partner in my salon. We established how much money was necessary each week to pay salon expenses. Each of us put in equal amounts and took the rest of the money via checks requiring both signatures to our individual bank accounts. It was a system devised before anything became an issue.

One subject that does not come up in most marriages with young people is retirement and long-range investments, etc. As I mentioned earlier, retirement comes sooner than we think and will cost more than we expect. Add to this conundrum the fact that one or both partners may become critically ill at some point, so those discussions need to take place. Although a negative thought at this point, if divorce occurs, having financial solvency eliminates some of the more difficult issues with which couples have to deal.

If it seems like I am making too much out of all of this, that would be partially right, but the inability to know the future makes these more vital issues. Remember that I have seen a few things first hand and among my friends. Being too quick to jump into a relationship that is this important is a big mistake. In fact, every few years the couple might need to have the "talks" again to see where they stand.

* * *

As I am completing this book, the world is experiencing a pandemic. America is making every effort to keep down the spread here, which has resulted in lost wages and scarcity of a few important products like toilet paper, and sanitizing cleaning products, and masks for health workers, etc. If you are reading this after that pandemic, you may be wondering why I mention toilet paper first—but you really don't want to know. Just thank God it is behind you. . . the pandemic, that is.

People who prepared financially will be able to survive. Those who either spent every paycheck from week to week or invested ALL or most of their savings in a 401K are singing the blues and living day to day in fear of their money running out. Wisdom in finances is second only to serving God through his Son, Jesus Christ.

Let's Talk about It

Third in the list of reasons for divorce, in my estimation, is a lack of communication. We hear this many times, but we often don't take it seriously. I look back on my 29-year marriage and see where I could have been more communicative. On the other hand, the other partner in any relationship might resist communication for fear of being criticized or humiliated (that's the real issue.)

People who are insecure or fearful tend to resist talking about or hearing what might be a problem, even though it might be the key to saving a relationship before it becomes too late to salvage it. As a result, we tend to put our guards up. It is the mark of distrust. If we do not trust the person to whom we have committed our lives to, who can we trust? It may be too late to trust the marriage counselor, but do allow a mediator to help clear the dust and the mud that develops over time when we fail to duke it out verbally. Cool heads need to prevail and openness is mandatory.

St. Paul's instructions in 1 Corinthians 7 go on to express the fact that a woman does not own her own body nor does the man. When we believe seriously that this is our covenant, we should treat each other as if they are our own souls—because they are. Emotional injury to the other is doing damage to one's own soul. What a mess we become then!

I saw a program that Barbara De Angelis, a leading expert on relationships and a highly respected leader in the field of personal growth, discussed an aspect of interpersonal relationships that has stuck with me for over 30 years. While I am using this as an example, I am not recommending her books because I haven't read any of them, so buyer beware.

She emphasizes how we harbor bad thoughts and feelings until our emotional tank gets so full that we will ultimately explode. The factor that caused the explosion may not even be relevant at the time of the explosion, but it is the thing that tops off the tank. Every time we hold back on expressing our feelings, we stuff it into the tank. By the time it explodes, it may be too late to salvage the relationship. It is far better to express an emotion or a feeling at the time rather than to let them accumulate and build up explosive energy.

One caution here: there are times and situations where we need to take a few moments to contemplate whether we might be wrong and check our actions/reactions. Forgiveness without delving into an argument might be the best cause of action. Forgiveness is paramount because it should eliminate the feelings that perpetrated it.

Often if I contemplate a matter, I find that I might be wrong, but I must decide whether to pursue the matter further to express that. Obviously, we cannot always make restitution and to keep an argument or heated discussion going can make the relationship one of constant haranguing and overly sensitive emotions. **We**

do not need to check our emotions at the door, but we are responsible for keeping them in check.

First and foremost rule in communication is to remember that the person to whom you have vowed to love and care for the rest of your life deserves your humility and selfless devotion. The LORD will bless that relationship.

Telephone, Television, and Technology

We might not think these subjects are relative to marriage counseling. Society's concentration on these three requires that we pay attention to the things on which we spend MOST of our time and energy .

The least of these might seem trivial, but I have seen people hurt and emotionally distraught over television, especially the choice of programs. I hear it over and over from wives who would like to spend time in the same room with their husbands but there is little choice in what they may have to watch. I understand why men wouldn't want to watch "chick-flicks" or the Hallmark Movie Channel, but there comes a time often when one should give up to maintain a happy relationship.

I dislike watching cop shows or the programs popular among men, like *Dirty Jobs*. These are obviously popular with men, but some compromises can be made with the DVR recording for a later time. When both mates are available to watch tv at the same time, considerations *need* to be made. Most men like to watch football, so there are situations when their wives can make other plans or go to another room to watch something else. How this works out is an individual thing, but both parties should be amenable to a solution. Failure to compromise may be the weak link in the marriage all the way around. Some men would rather, or at least threaten to, leave the room when they cannot choose the programs.

The separation of the couple every evening after dinner is a dangerous precedent and will ultimately result in emotional separation. The advent of the remote control becomes an issue in some relationships for two reasons. It enables the person "in control" to keep changing channels when commercials come on or when he/she has not decided on a program. Or, worse still, is the watcher who thinks he/she can watch two or three programs at one time. The remote control becomes public enemy number one.

The telephone, whether hand-held or on the wall as it was in my younger days, is a couple divider and an intrusion into the mind of the person not on the phone. Some men hate to have their wives on the phone when they are home because it is a disturbance, but more often than not, it takes away from the couple time. If the couple NOT on the phone could have some insecurity issues that are accelerated during those times. I can't imagine how insecurities are handled with our obsession with the phone when other people are sitting at elbow's length.

Having been a stay-at-home mom during many years of my children's lives, I spent time visiting with friends on the phone, but I knew to get off the phone when the family was gathered after school and work. My friends also had meals to prepare and families to engage. Men are often jealous creatures and don't like to share their wives once they are home from work. This jealousy might also arise when children enter the family, but we can discuss that later.

Then there are the people (men and women) who are apt to talk on the phone in the evening when they come home from work. Depending on the conversation and where it takes place, these episodes can be disturbing. Always consider the other people in the house when talking on the phone at home and in stores or restaurants.

We've all seen the examples of both men and women constantly on the phone with work. Since when does a person's having a full-time phone have to conduct business even after business hours are over?--certainly a fly in the ointment of the 21st century business man or woman.

One man expressed to me that his wife was cheerful when she answered the phone but did not use the same "voice" in her conversation with him. Consequently, he became angry when the phone rang during dinnertime. This may be a rule to observe during family time. That man's issue might be a matter of actually listening to see the distinction before giving counsel. Listening can be in the ear of the beholder.

I gave my cell phone number to my college students, especially those online. However, I made it clear that a text message was my choice for them to be precise regarding their questions. Longer discussions needed to be reserved for normal business day schedules. Emails had their drawbacks in that they were not so immediate.

Coming into the twenty-first century, we have a whole new bag of problems with cell phones. Who knew fifty years ago that we would not only carry our phones around with us but that we would also be addicted to them? I still find myself wondering how people have that much to say to another human, especially when the room is full of live people.

People walk on the street giving their phones full attention; I've seen men and women doing this while there were children in their charge who might easily have gotten into traffic or snatched by a stranger. This is insane behavior and could be a major breakdown of relationships with spouses and children. If a person would endanger their lives and that of their children while checking online on their phones, what hope would they have of creating a good relationship at home?

I heard recently on the national news that the numbers have skyrocketed in the last few years for pedestrian deaths due to distracted drivers and walkers absorbed in their cell phones. Failing to pay attention is costing our lives.

On the recent episode of *Married at First Sight*, two of the women entered into serious discussions with their spouse about their relationships while holding, watching, and scanning their cell phones—not even looking up. One of them picked the cell phone up and carried it to hug her husband when the argument had reached a conclusion. After the hug with her arm still around his neck and sitting in his lap, she went back to looking down at her phone. This is worse than absurd; it is downright inhuman activity. It says, "I care more about the trivial information I'm scrolling than I do about you." Unacceptable.

Children and often young people actually don't know any better but adults should seize the problem and wake up to the reality that relationships don't just happen, but they can be wrecked by inattention.

The same ideas apply to computers—primarily because the internet is on our hand-held cell phones. Being on a PC is problematic for some of the same reasons except that they might actually cause a person to be in another room apart from the spouse and the family. I knew this would be a problem when we bought our first computer even before the Superhighway was built and we were connected.

While the internet has become a wealth of good information, it has also become the greatest menace and threat to our safety. Caution should be exercised at all times. Social media is a good place to find and interact with friends but it is not a substitute for spouses, children, families, and friends. These types of addictions should be dealt with exactly like drug or alcohol addictions.

Worse than being alone is the rejection when one is in the same room with people who are supposed to love them. This goes for both husbands and wives—later with children. These problems are regularly addressed on social media, but I don't think people are seizing the opportunity to take the internet/cell phones out of the relationships that mean the most.

Perhaps the best solution for adults and children is to set up some guidelines for use. Many people use computers all day at work but continue to give them their personal lives after work. Divided emotions can be curbed if we first realize what we have accepted as our new "norm." It is called "obsession" and there are ways of dealing with the psychological, emotional, and physical danger.

Before I leave this subject, let me address one of the dangers that relate to both internet obsession and sex. When I was a child, our only exposure to sex was in magazines like *True Confessions*. (I think that is one of the titles.) In any case, children were not allowed to read them. Even then we had to imagine things from the innuendoes. On occasion a kid in the neighborhood would try to educate us and make us ask questions about sex—but it was always taboo. An occasional girl in school would be tagged as "loose," but they were few and far between. My mother didn't even use the word "pregnant" in a polite society; she used "PG" and referred to her maternity clothes as "hatching jackets."

While you may be laughing at that absurdity, let me remind you that sexual violence, human trafficking, and child sexual predators have increased beyond our ability to control it any longer. Most of that increase is directly related to internet sites and the lax television standards for decency. There are free websites where we can see every kind of sex explicitly. Children should not be allowed to engage in social media where grown men can entice them to meet up with them, but these predators find a way because it is available and parents are not paying attention.

Our schools aren't helping because they are training grounds for sexual laxity and immoral behavior that not only threatens the morality of our nation but the minds of our vulnerable children. Children are being taught and encouraged to believe things they are not ready for, lifestyles inconsistent with their mental health as children. We need to save those discussions for the time when they can analyze and make their own decisions. I'm not speaking solely as a political opinion but as one who is concerned about the health of our families and our nation.

People, our heads are not stuck in the sand; they are stuck in the internet. The difference: we cannot see anything in the sand, but there is a plethora of images to hook us on the internet while we are not paying attention to what is going on around us; then we are completely blinded and getting angry when someone confronts us.

Love and Marriage

Like the old song says, "Love and marriage go together like a horse and carriage. . . you can't have one without the other." Love is not necessary for two people to get married, but like the carriage without the horse, the going would be rough if only "driven" by 2 people trying to move it; that can be done because it does have wheels, after all. Moving a carriage by humans and trying to make it move in a forward motion is not only difficult but it is hysterical to watch.

The necessary component is love, but not everything called love fits the bill. Love is the most misunderstood word in the English language, partly because there is only one word we use for it. In the Greek language, there are at least 3. Initially, most understandings are related to the *philia* or brotherly love and *eros*, the more physical or sexual feelings.

Neither of those cases is likely to fulfill the lasting results needed for long and happy marriages. The *agape* love is that purest form of love that we receive from God, the Father. When humans come to the point of loving the person to whom we are bound either by family relations or marriage without reservation or condition, their successful marriage is possible. That kind of love is spelled out rather succinctly in Paul's letter to the Corinthian church, a church where the "new" church was having difficulties. The Corinthian church was having some difficulty blending in with the *new* concept of a relationship to the "Hebrew" God. Paul lays it out very plainly in 1 Corinthians:

> 3 If I give all I possess to the poor and give over my body to hardship that I may boast, but do not have love, I gain nothing.
>
> 4 Love is patient, love is kind. It does not envy, it does not boast, it is not proud. 5 It does not dishonor others, it is not self-seeking, it is not

easily angered, it keeps no record of wrongs. 6 Love does not delight in evil but rejoices with the truth. 7 It always protects, always trusts, always hopes, always perseveres.

8 *Love never fails*. [Emphasis mine.]

(1 Cor. 13:3-8 KJV)

These points are related directly to both partners in a marriage relationship. When one partner in a marriage falls short of this goal, the marriage is destined to fail at its weakest link. Before a couple makes the decision and all of the plans that go into a wedding ceremony, these points need to be acknowledged. The couple should recognize that this is the ultimate goal. I do not think it is humanly possible to know or understand what all of this means until the marriage becomes an everyday practice, but the goal is to work toward this.

I include this portion of scripture in the marriage ceremony because the couple is agreeing to work toward the fulfillment of a love contract commanded by God and sealed by God. Agape love is the kind of love that only

God can give; but it is his desire to give it to all people who belong to him.

One way to keep these "love vows" is to remember them when the going gets rough. Scripture tells us not to let the sun go down on our wrath; when we argue before bed, the argument festers in the subconscious all night and the opposing parties are apt to wake up with a wall erected between them. Settling the matter before this happens is primary. Doing this may be more difficult for one person than the other, but the result affects both.

There is a much longer teaching that could be inserted here about forgiveness, but I am going to shorten it by saying that forgiveness is not only necessary but it is mandatory in human relationships. The refusal to grant forgiveness puts a wedge between that person and God. Jesus reminded us that if we don't forgive others, God will not forgive us. I don't know about any of you, but I don't want to be on that side of a relationship to the Eternal and Almighty God. Forgiveness may be the only solution to arguments or fights any time during the day but especially at night. Don't set yourself up for failure by holding out on forgiveness with your mate. Nothing is worth losing your soul over.

This text is not actually about divorce per se, but let me say that going through divorce, even uncontested, breeds many sources for anger and bitterness. No matter what, do not let unforgiveness get planted at the root of your soul. Cool heads need to prevail in arguments before the situation comes to divorce and that is where the love factor must preside.

One underlying factor that breeds an unlovable marriage is selfishness and a need to be in control. Both partners have desires, habits, shortcomings, and lifestyles as a single person, but each one has to face those and be willing to compromise. Okay, I have said it, "Compromise." I am sure that word has come up in life before, but it is more important than ever in marriage.

The need for compromise may be as simple as what television programs to watch; who is going to be responsible for cooking or cleaning or both; who is going to handle the bank account; who is going to pay the bills; where will you go on vacation; with whose family will you spend the holidays? These are not things most couples have encountered before they "fall in love" or start considering getting married. At my age and in my experience as having been married and now dating, I can tell you certain things become more apparent when you have had experience in compromising situations. For example, I have said jokingly that I am not giving up my tv remote control EVER to another human being. While people might laugh when I say that, I am quite serious; this is probably why I will not consider joining with another human who has to live under my roof. When couples have to go to separate rooms to watch television, which is the most common form of daily entertainment, the marriage suffers an irreconcilable rift. With cell phone addictions, the problem is worse because people are often in the same room but not connecting emotionally.

A seemingly less serious matter is the personal habits of the one to whom a person is planning to spend a life together. Personal hygiene is a biggy with me. That begins with the hair, face, and nails; how a person appears in public tells the tale. I dated a man who insisted on taking a shower just before he met me for the date; his hair was still wet most of the time when he first arrived and he always smelled so good—though not overwhelmingly so. Older men who have long, white "boar" hairs growing out of places on their face aside from the beard make me think, "I just couldn't kiss that face!" Okay, guys, they aren't that hard to remove with a pair of tweezers! The other things that stand out are dirty fingernails! If the other person doesn't understand how unsightly and nasty their dirty fingernails are, what else are they missing? These are just the things the other person can see!

In counseling sessions I ask couples to point out a few of those things. Some things one person can ultimately live with but others are apt to cause a problem over time. Let's consider how the individuals live insofar as their physical surroundings are concerned. For example, are they organized to a fault, a trait that could cause a "messy" to get frustrated or vice versa?

My point in bringing up these issues is to suggest that failure to handle them ahead of time could create a chasm that will prevent real love from growing and blossoming in the marriage.

Last but not least is the necessity for respecting your partner in life. Becoming sensitive to what hurts your partner and reading their deeply held insecurities will help you willfully avoid doing or saying anything to hurt them further. Sometimes we get so close to a person and that person has been the source of hurt feelings in the past that we become insensitive.

I'm going to tell only one story about my post-divorce relationship with my ex-husband. In a conversation with him in which I was trying to understand our dynamics, I mentioned, "What if I criticized your job or your salary. . ."

He didn't let me finish the sentence before declaring, "Oh, I didn't make enough money?!"

I honestly never, ever felt that he was not providing for me or our family but I knew how sensitive men are about their jobs so I was about to make a point.

Honestly, I always felt very secure financially and in other ways; however, what he thought I was saying scratched a raw nerve. He took it as a criticism that he thought I was harboring.

This is a very good reason to have honest and calm conversations on a regular basis. Your spouse should always feel secure in your feelings and love for them to the point of appreciating all that they bring to the marriage.

Love will find a way and will help you read an honest and sincere feeling toward each other. As I said earlier, keeping fears, anxieties, and angers pent up will cause an explosion of the proportions that no one can put them back together.

If your partner misreads you, it is because one of you is being insecure or dishonest. Keep those lines of communication open at all cost.

Watch and Learn

Observing people's behavior is a trait we are often missing out on with the addiction or obsession with technology or crazy television programs that are teaching bad behavior—even in comedy programs. I have been doing a lot of close observation related to married couples of late.

The program *Married at First Sight* has me hooked and keeps me almost spellbound each week. I have become a student of human behavior because of my various professions, so this program has allowed me to improve my counseling strategies.

While I'm on the subject somewhat of love, let me use the example from last week's program. First let me tell you something about the program in case you don't know. Couples are chosen by a panel of experts based on questionnaires and interviews. This season 5 couples have been paired up to marry a partner whom they have never seen until they walk down the aisle or stand beside the preacher. I'll skip all of the oddities of such a thing and go on to explain that a camera crew follows the couples around, even in their bedrooms, for 8 weeks and then the couples will decide whether to remain married or get a divorce.

This practice of "arranged marriages" is not as strange as it may seem to 21st century people. Last week, for my example, one of the couples had an interview with one of the experts after coming "home" from their honeymoon. The subject of love came up. The response of the husband was not pleasing to the wife and she has been misbehaving ever since. What I want to say to her is what I will say to my readers and counselees.

First of all, the groom said he had never been in love although he is into his 20s. I personally don't think that is strange at all; first of all, most of us misrepresent or misinterpret when we think we are "in love." If we misinterpret being in love as being sexually or even emotionally attracted, it is sure to cause the bride who has only known this guy for 2 weeks some emotional pain. I want to say to her, "Get a grip! Give him a minute to catch his breath." This particular couple was the first to admit to having sex, which was not required, the first few nights they were married as complete strangers. Now when he says he may not be able to say that he is in love in 8 weeks, she is acting like a spoiled child. By the way, there were signs that this young woman may be quite frisky to begin with, so she may be totally confused and their communication is missing the mark considerably.

Listening to his comments about his thoughts on being in love, I can tell he has been hurt before in the past when he thought he was in love though it turned out to be a flighty, perhaps sexual, thing. No matter how good the sex may be, it does not translate to the agape, long-lasting kind of devotion required to keep the marriage going. I'm disappointed that the experts aren't saying this to the couple. "Woman! Just give him time!"

Her lack of understanding has put some serious barriers to an otherwise great beginning. The program is in the 7th week now and she is behaving badly a lot—like a spoiled child. I will be surprised if they remain married.

Sex may be great for starters, but sex won't hold a marriage together without agape love explained in 1 Corinthians 13. There are plenty of unexpected issues that come up in the bedroom that can bust the marriage into pieces if that is all the marriage is built upon. People have to have real lives outside of the bedroom that requires much more emotion and physical restraint than sex.

One more point from that show before I shift subjects: one of the husbands has said to his wife that he is not attracted to her; naturally it has caused her great consternation as she translates it to mean that he does not find her attractive, which is understandable. However, when you hear him talk about it, he uses another word that should settle her down a bit—though it hasn't because no one is explaining.

But let me try: he says there hasn't been any "chemistry." On several occasions, he says she is very pretty and she is athletic, which matches him perfectly. On the other hand, chemistry is something he is searching for with a complete stranger. Chemistry, from my way of thinking, is different from being attracted to someone. One is dependent upon an emotional/psychic connection that is not dependent upon the way a person looks; it is an inner knowing or comfort level that the husband in this case has not experienced yet. Both chemistry and attraction may be necessary for this husband to "feel" before he consummates the marriage—and he may never feel that with her no matter how beautiful she may be. Like the other wife, she just needs to give it some more time. Last week's episode indicates they are making more of an effort to do what most couples do before they marry—become "bonded." This could be a marriage that continues after the 8 weeks if time and experience brings him to the place he wants or feels he should be. Unfortunately, they never reach that place because they aren't communicating effectively.

It may seem the love chapter should be among the first; however, there is so much misunderstanding about this subject that I wanted to save it till the end to get the readers undivided attention.

The Best Prescription for Marriage

I have saved the very best counsel for the very last so that couples can see that anything else will be a struggle and might cause the marriage to be in trouble before it has had a solid beginning.

That subject is the marriage ordained by and supported by the LORD Himself. I take my responsibility seriously when I officiate at a wedding and will not accept the responsibility for uniting couples who do not individually and as a couple accept Christ as their personal savior. Marriage is a sacred obligation not to be entered into inadvisably or lightly.

Asking the LORD to bless your union is a forever commitment to serve Him and follow His guidance. Anything else is treading on unsteady ground. There are people in this world who are naturally kind and respectful of their mates and children, but the eternal benefits do not last beyond death if their souls are not saved. They also cannot teach their families (wives and children) to love and serve the LORD nor do they have the desire to do so.

Before I begin the marriage counseling sessions, I inquire as to the commitment to do the LORD's will in their relationship—to keep the vows they will be making during the ceremony. To those whom do not take the commitment seriously, I do not accept responsibility. I recommend they choose another officiate.

Today, as you read this text, examine yourself before the LORD and make the commitment to do all that is within your power to work on this relationship and the later introduction of children. I am always available to counsel now or after the marriage, but there are good Christian counselors available to help.

Author's Bio and Last Words

For all of the important issues related to marriage, counseling is necessary before and after marriage. While many couples skip the counseling because of the lack of will to do the work or a failure to understand the importance, it could be the difference between a happy and a miserable commitment. Once the counseling and the wedding are over, I am no longer responsible; however, I am available for further counseling. Couples may contact me through my email address, dellbelew33@hotmail.com or by phone—a number which I will give at the time of counseling.

Counseling can be the best beginning of the happiest of marriages.

I want to give some biographical information about myself. I was married for 29 years and one month. I cannot go into all of my own joys and trials, but I can assure couples that I learned a great deal from having been through those years and, especially the post-divorce depression and since. Having survived, I have much wisdom about the ins and outs of couple relationships enough to tell couples that even when we do our best, some personality issues that go unchecked can wreck a relationship no matter how much you may have been paying attention.

The Holy Spirit is the teacher about all things we call LIFE. I have been a committed Christian for 45 years and a student of the Bible and called to be a Teacher. I am ordained by The Missionary Church International since the 1990s. Before that I was a local pastor in the United Methodist Church, having served a total of 4 churches in Georgia and Pennsylvania. I attended seminary at Erskine Theological Seminary and Pittsburgh Theological Seminary toward a Master's of Divinity degree.

Before all of the above, I received a doctorate in English from The University of Georgia in 1994. I have taught English at Brewton-Parker College, Waynesburg University, Savannah State University, Armstrong State University, and South College. I taught English, Religion, Humanities, and Professional Writing at Strayer University. I retired in 2015.

In my retirement years, I have published 4 or the 21 books to date. I have published 117 videotapes on my YouTube channel, most of them art tutorials or painting demonstrations. As you can see, I have been very busy during retirement.

This text is book 21. I also have a website www.dellbelew.com where you can find a variety of subjects including my paintings.

Being a good student of the Bible in my relationship to the LORD Jesus Christ, I have learned a great deal from the Master of Love and Marriage that I am always happy to impart to couples seeking the God kind of marriage.

May the LORD bless and keep you and make His face to shine upon you now and forevermore. Amen!

NOTES